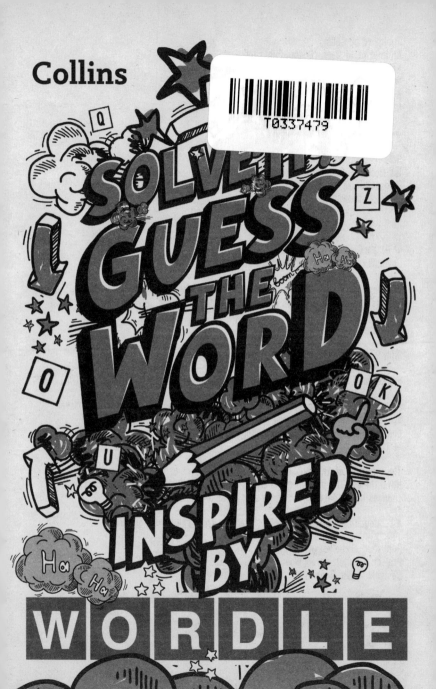

Published by Collins
An imprint of HarperCollins Publishers
HarperCollins Publishers
Westerhill Road
Bishopbriggs
Glasgow G64 2QT

www.harpercollins.co.uk

HarperCollins Publishers
1st Floor. Watermarque Building
Ringsend Road
Dublin 4. Ireland

10 9 8 7 6 5 4 3

ISBN 978-0-00-855548-1

Printed and bound in the UK using 100% renewable electricity at CPI Group (UK) Ltd

Publisher: Michelle l'Anson
Project Manager: Sarah Woods
Designer: Kevin Robbins

With more than 140 puzzles, you'll
never want to put this book down!

Play this fun word game with friends or family
and take it in turns to see how quickly
you can guess the word.

All you need is a pen or pencil to play.

With hints on the page or at the back of the
book if you want more of a challenge. there is space to write
down your scores and a handy score chart!

So... are you ready to

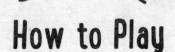

How to Play

This is a game for two players. The object of the game is to guess the word in six tries.

1. Player 1 checks what the word is at the back of the book.

2. Player 2 guesses a word and writes it into the first line of the grid.

3. Player 1 draws a circle around any letters that are in the answer word in the correct place.

They draw a square around any letters that are in the answer word but in the wrong place.

They put a X on any letters that are not in the answer word on the alphabet grid at the bottom of the page.

4. Player 2 guesses the word again and adds it to the next line of the grid.

5. Play continues. Player 2 has six tries to guess the word.

6. Player 2 scores points depending on how many tries they guessed the word in. e.g. if they guessed the word in 3 tries they get 3 points. The aim is to get as low a score as possible!

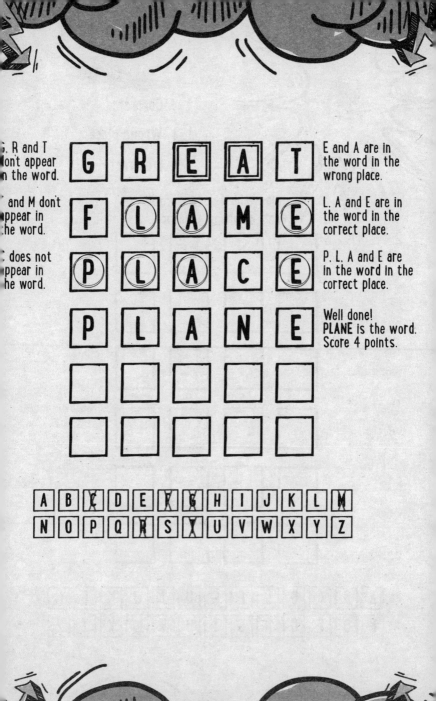

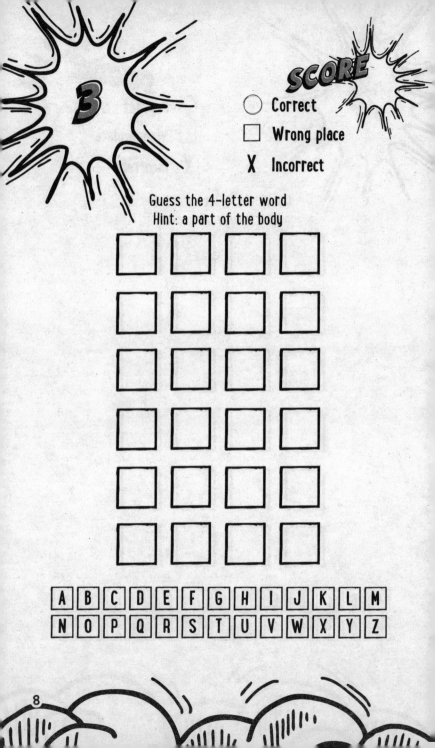

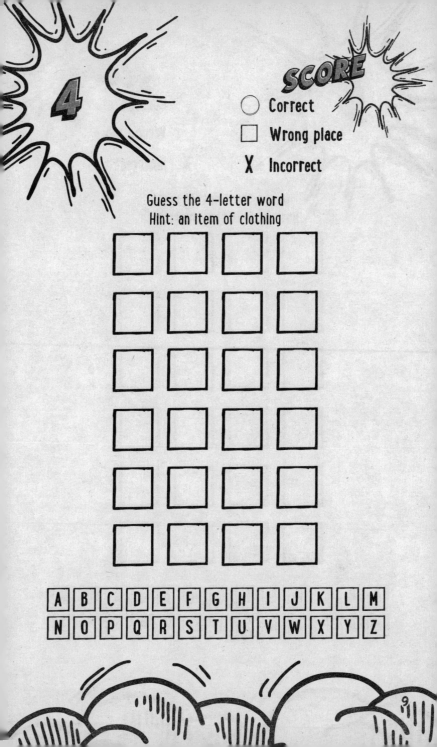

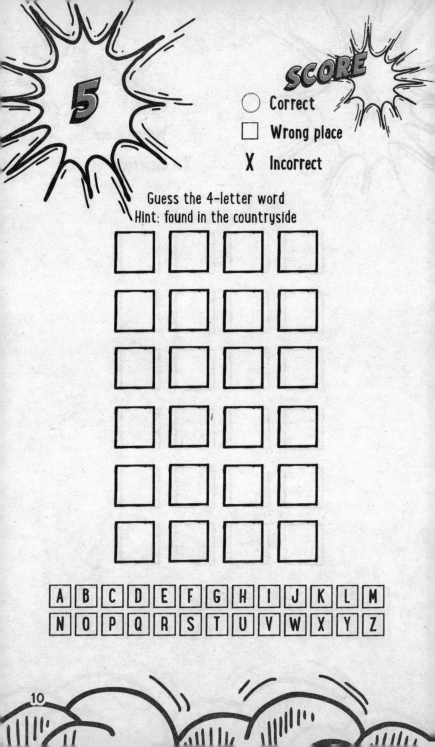

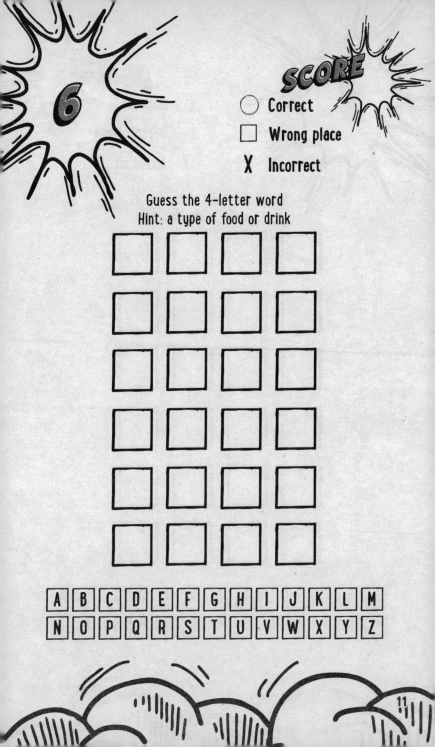

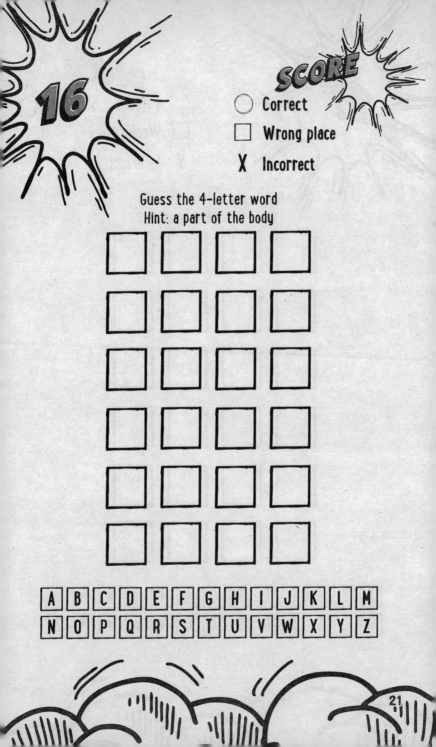

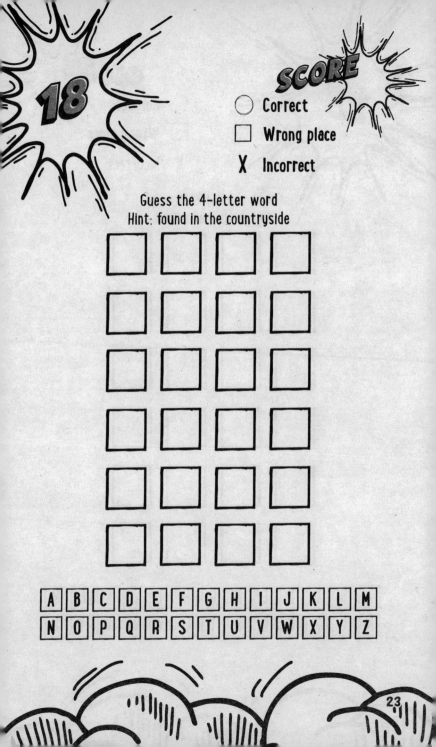

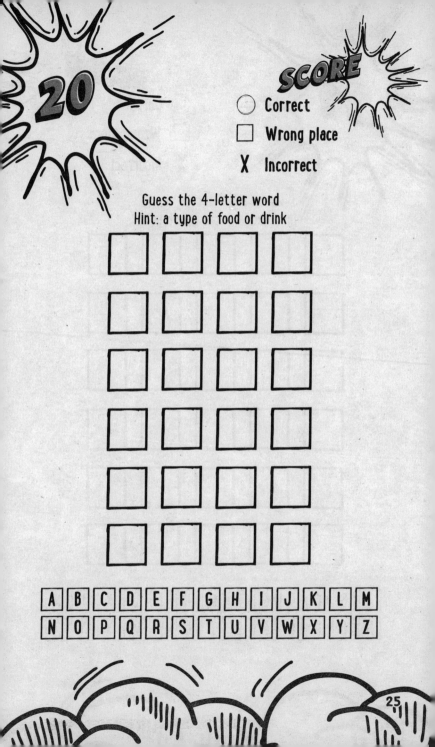

21

○ Correct
□ Wrong place
X Incorrect

Guess the 5-letter word
Hint: found in the countryside

| A | B | C | D | E | F | G | H | I | J | K | L | M |
| N | O | P | Q | R | S | T | U | V | W | X | Y | Z |

30

SCORE
○ Correct
□ Wrong place
X Incorrect

Guess the 5-letter word
Hint: found in the countryside

A B C D E F G H I J K L M
N O P Q R S T U V W X Y Z

35

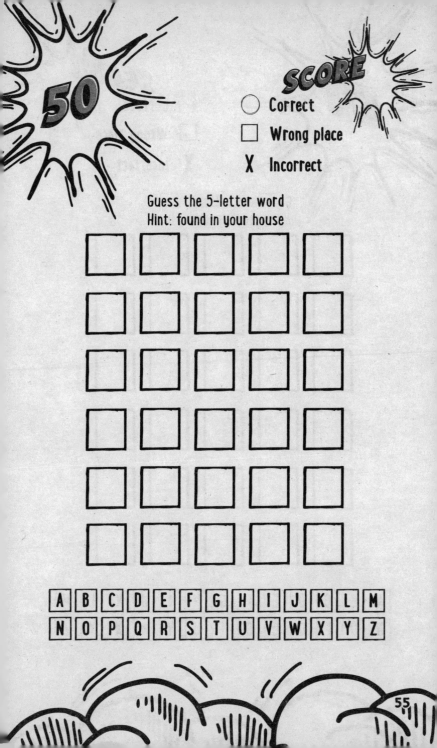

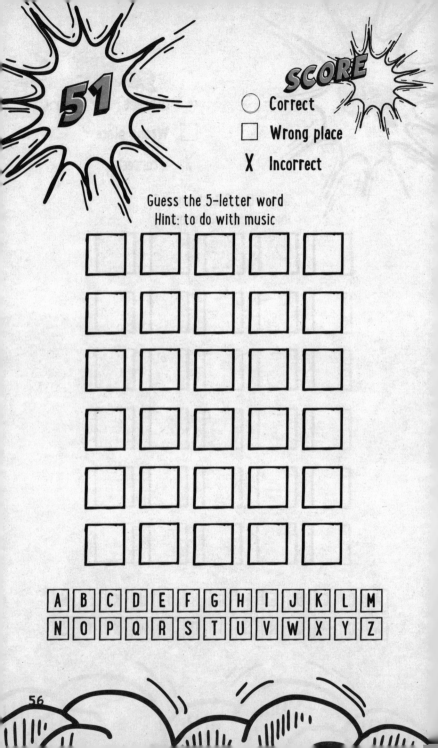

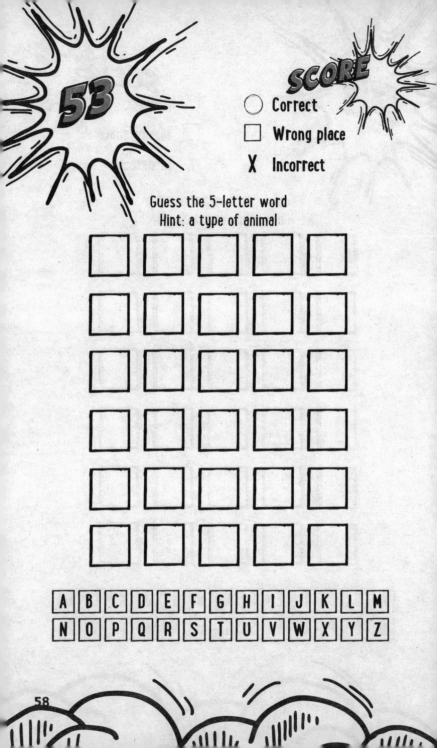

63

SCORE

○ Correct

□ Wrong place

X Incorrect

Guess the 5-letter word
Hint: found in the countryside

A B C D E F G H I J K L M
N O P Q R S T U V W X Y Z

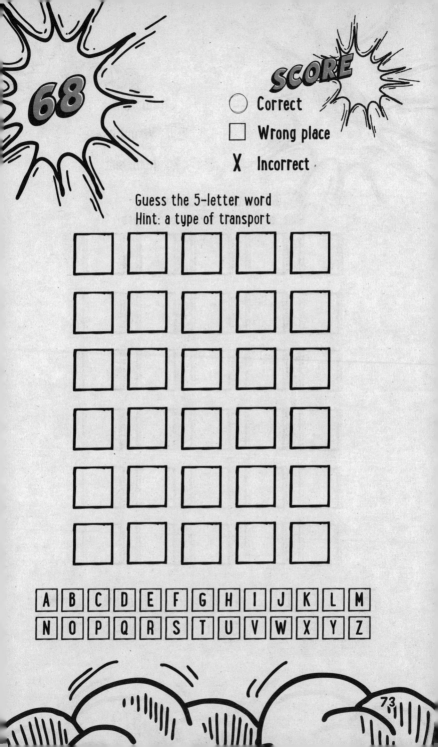

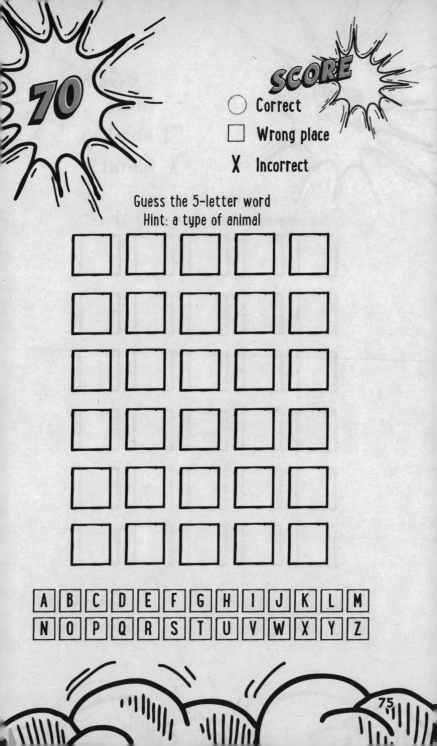

77

SCORE
- ○ Correct
- □ Wrong place
- X Incorrect

Guess the 5-letter word
You can ask for a hint if you would like one.

| A | B | C | D | E | F | G | H | I | J | K | L | M |
| N | O | P | Q | R | S | T | U | V | W | X | Y | Z |

80

SCORE

○ Correct

□ Wrong place

X Incorrect

Guess the 5-letter word
You can ask for a hint if you would like one.

A B C D E F G H I J K L M
N O P Q R S T U V W X Y Z

85

84

SCORE

◯ Correct

▢ Wrong place

X Incorrect

Guess the 5-letter word
You can ask for a hint if you would like one.

| A | B | C | D | E | F | G | H | I | J | K | L | M |
| N | O | P | Q | R | S | T | U | V | W | X | Y | Z |

87

SCORE

○ Correct

☐ Wrong place

X Incorrect

Guess the 5-letter word
You can ask for a hint if you would like one.

A B C D E F G H I J K L M
N O P Q R S T U V W X Y Z

90

SCORE
○ Correct
□ Wrong place
X Incorrect

Guess the 5-letter word
You can ask for a hint if you would like one.

A B C D E F G H I J K L M
N O P Q R S T U V W X Y Z

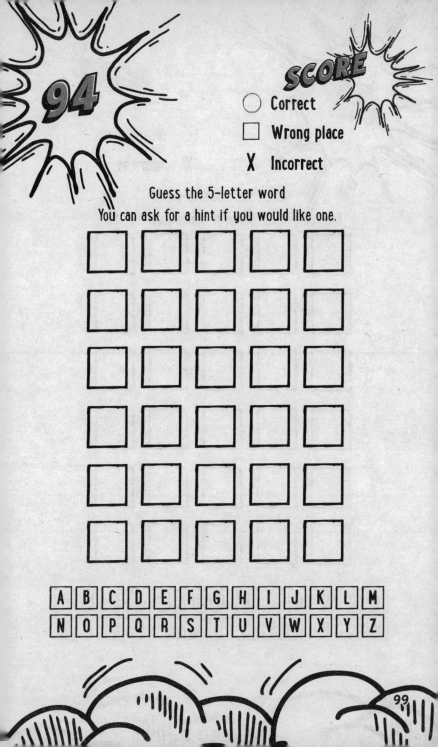

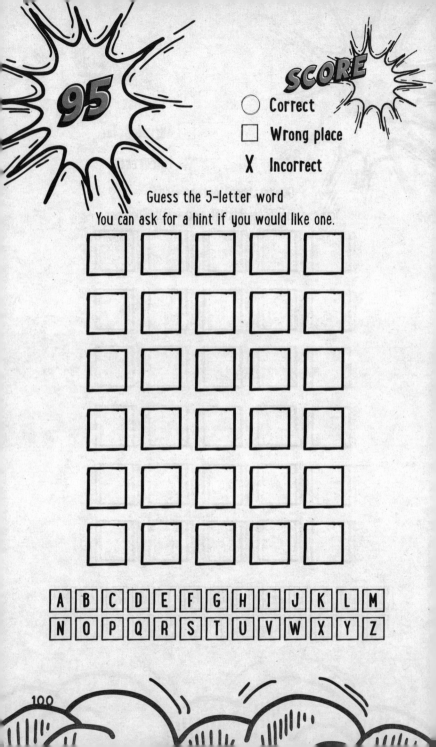

97

SCORE

◯ Correct

☐ Wrong place

X Incorrect

Guess the 5-letter word
You can ask for a hint if you would like one.

| A | B | C | D | E | F | G | H | I | J | K | L | M |
| N | O | P | Q | R | S | T | U | V | W | X | Y | Z |

99

SCORE

○ Correct
□ Wrong place
X Incorrect

Guess the 5-letter word
You can ask for a hint if you would like one.

A B C D E F G H I J K L M
N O P Q R S T U V W X Y Z

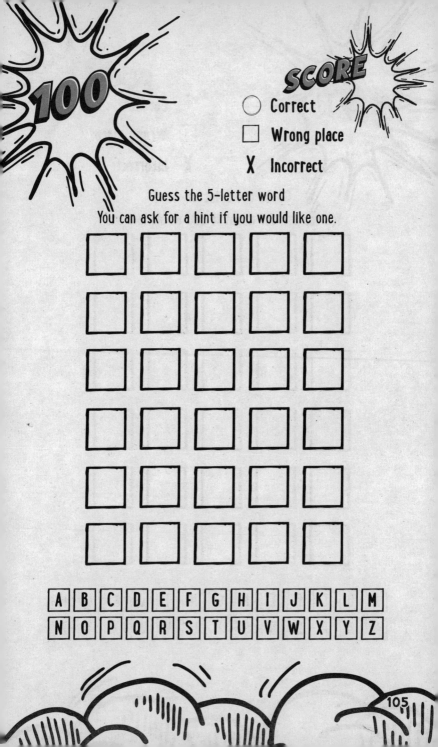

100

SCORE

◯ Correct

☐ Wrong place

✗ Incorrect

Guess the 5-letter word
You can ask for a hint if you would like one.

A B C D E F G H I J K L M
N O P Q R S T U V W X Y Z

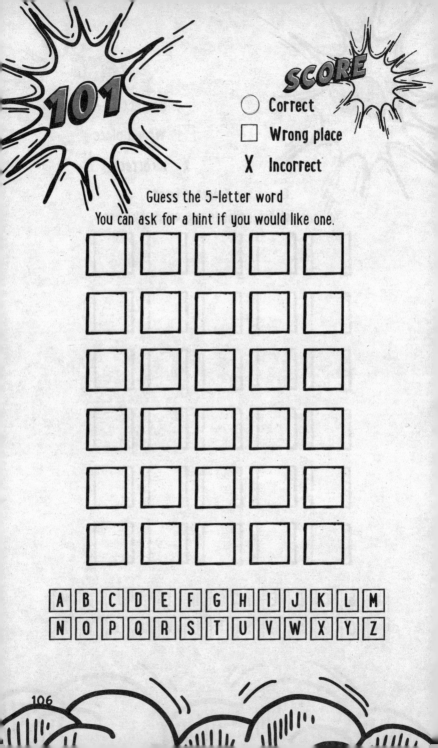

101

SCORE
◯ Correct
☐ Wrong place
X Incorrect

Guess the 5-letter word
You can ask for a hint if you would like one.

A B C D E F G H I J K L M
N O P Q R S T U V W X Y Z

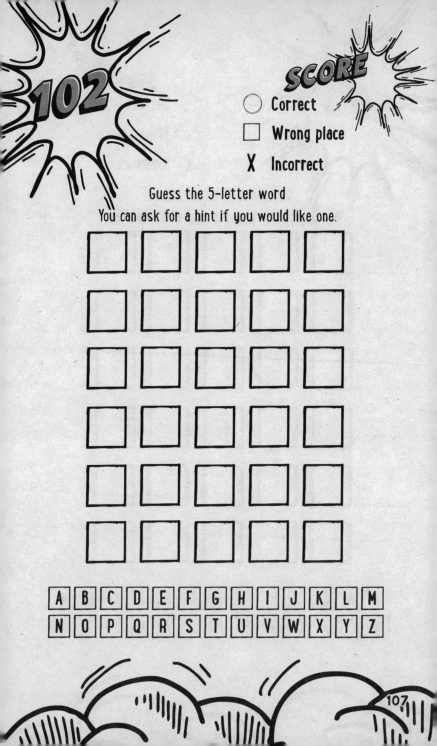

103

SCORE

◯ Correct
▢ Wrong place
X Incorrect

Guess the 5-letter word
You can ask for a hint if you would like one.

| A | B | C | D | E | F | G | H | I | J | K | L | M |
| N | O | P | Q | R | S | T | U | V | W | X | Y | Z |

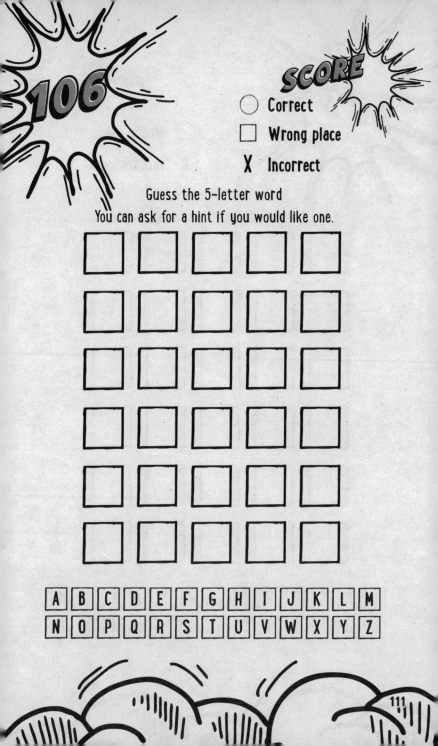

110

SCORE
○ Correct
□ Wrong place
X Incorrect

Guess the 5-letter word
You can ask for a hint if you would like one.

A B C D E F G H I J K L M
N O P Q R S T U V W X Y Z

111

SCORE

○ Correct

□ Wrong place

X Incorrect

Guess the 5-letter word
You can ask for a hint if you would like one.

| A | B | C | D | E | F | G | H | I | J | K | L | M |
| N | O | P | Q | R | S | T | U | V | W | X | Y | Z |

125

SCORE

◯ Correct

☐ Wrong place

X Incorrect

Guess the 5-letter word
There is no hint so see if you can work it out!

| A | B | C | D | E | F | G | H | I | J | K | L | M |
| N | O | P | Q | R | S | T | U | V | W | X | Y | Z |

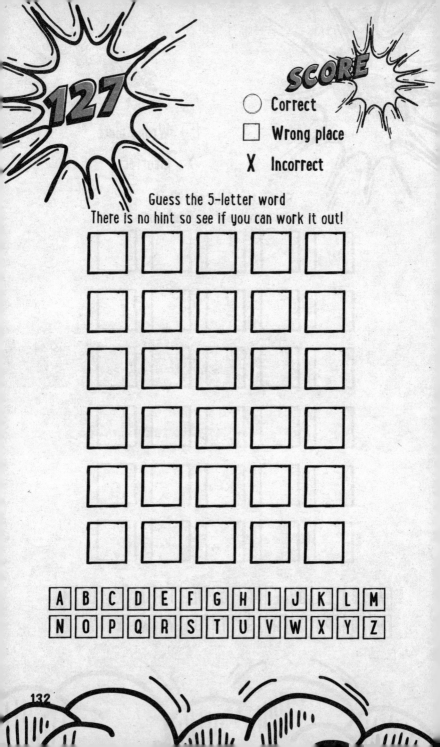

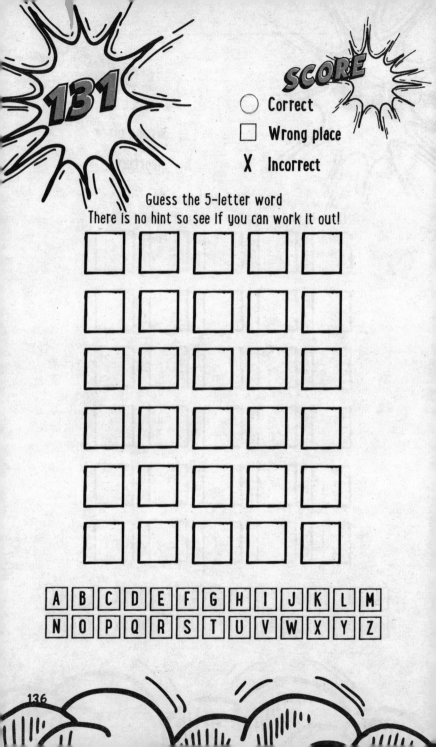

138

SCORE

○ Correct
□ Wrong place
X Incorrect

Guess the 5-letter word
There is no hint so see if you can work it out!

| A | B | C | D | E | F | G | H | I | J | K | L | M |
| N | O | P | Q | R | S | T | U | V | W | X | Y | Z |

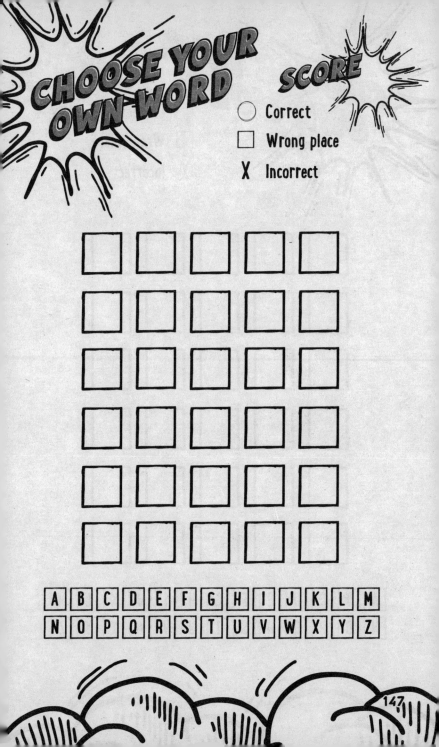

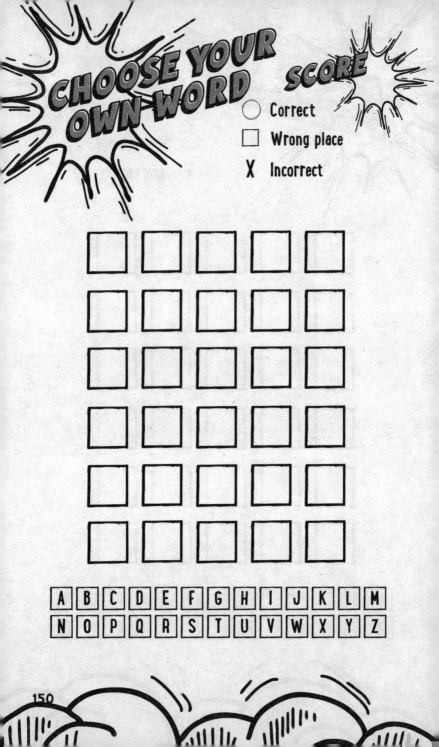

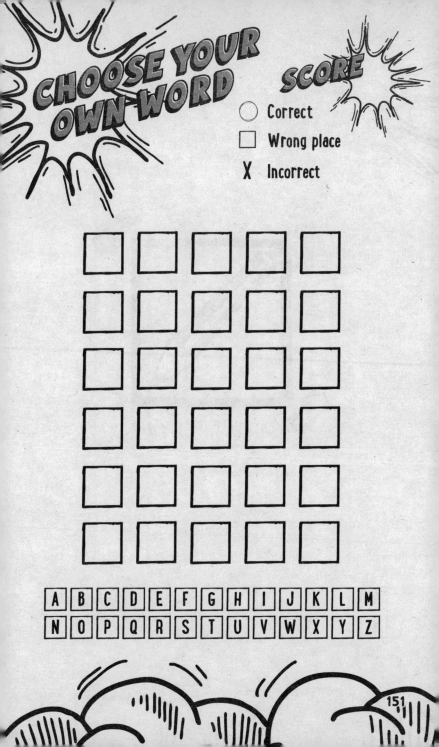

The answers have been separated into odd numbered puzzles e.g. 1, 3, 5 and even numbered puzzles. e.g. 2, 4, 6 so that you don't see the answer to the next puzzle. This would spoil the fun of the game! For answers to even numbered puzzles go to page 157.

ODD NUMBERED PUZZLES

Puzzle 1	Puzzle 3	Puzzle 5
SHIP	HEAD	TREE
Puzzle 7	Puzzle 9	Puzzle 11
GOLF	DRUM	BOOT
Puzzle 13	Puzzle 15	Puzzle 17
KICK	SWIM	HORN
Puzzle 19	Puzzle 21	Puzzle 23
WOLF	PETAL	CHESS
Puzzle 25	Puzzle 27	Puzzle 29
COACH	CAMEL	DRESS
Puzzle 31	Puzzle 33	Puzzle 35
ANGRY	DANCE	PLANE
Puzzle 37	Puzzle 39	Puzzle 41
CLEAN	ZEBRA	ELBOW
Puzzle 43	Puzzle 45	Puzzle 47
DAISY	EMPTY	CHIME
Puzzle 49	Puzzle 51	Puzzle 53
TOAST	OPERA	PANDA

Puzzle 55
CHEST

Puzzle 57
TIGER

Puzzle 59
FIELD

Puzzle 61
FUNNY

Puzzle 63
RIVER

Puzzle 65
ORGAN

Puzzle 67
KAYAK

Puzzle 69
PRESS

Puzzle 71
THUMB
Hint: a part
of the body

Puzzle 73
HOLLY
Hint: found in
the countryside

Puzzle 75
GRAPE
Hint: a type of
food or drink

Puzzle 77
SKATE
Hint: to do with
hobbies or sports

Puzzle 79
TABLE
Hint: found in
your house

Puzzle 81
CHEEK
Hint: a part
of the body

Puzzle 83
SALAD
Hint: a type of
food or drink

Puzzle 85
PIANO
Hint: to do
with music

Puzzle 87
GLOVE
Hint: an item
of clothing

Puzzle 89
SPOON
Hint: found in
your house

Puzzle 91
SQUID
Hint: a type
of animal

Puzzle 93
UPSET
Hint: a describing
word (adjective)

Puzzle 95
PASTA
Hint: a type of
food or drink

Puzzle 97
HEART
Hint: a part
of the body

Puzzle 99
VIOLA
Hint: to do
with music

Puzzle 101

LAUGH

Hint: a doing or
action word (verb)

Puzzle 103

MOLAR

Hint: a part
of the body

Puzzle 105

YACHT

Hint: a type
of transport

Puzzle 107

QUILT

Hint: found in
your house

Puzzle 109

BARGE

Hint: a type
of transport

Puzzle 111

YEAST

Hint: a type of
food or drink

Puzzle 113

WEIGH

Hint: a doing or
action word (verb)

Puzzle 115

WAGON

Hint: a type
of transport

Puzzle 117

JUICY

Hint: a describing
word (adjective)

Puzzle 119

WHISK

Hint: found in
your house

Puzzle 121

CHILD

Puzzle 123

HOUSE

Puzzle 125

ADULT

Puzzle 127

LEMON

Puzzle 129

KNOCK

Puzzle 131

BLANK

Puzzle 133

UNDER

Puzzle 135

CRASH

Puzzle 137

SHAKE

Puzzle 139

NIGHT

EVEN NUMBERED PUZZLES

Puzzle 2	Puzzle 4	Puzzle 6
FISH	SOCK	CAKE

Puzzle 8	Puzzle 10	Puzzle 12
SINK	BIKE	VASE

Puzzle 14	Puzzle 16	Puzzle 18
BAKE	NOSE	ROCK

Puzzle 20	Puzzle 22	Puzzle 24
MEAT	TRAIN	JEANS

Puzzle 26	Puzzle 28	Puzzle 30
BRUSH	MOUTH	GRASS

Puzzle 32	Puzzle 34	Puzzle 36
BREAD	GLASS	FLUTE

Puzzle 38	Puzzle 40	Puzzle 42
HORSE	TWIST	SKIRT

Puzzle 44	Puzzle 46	Puzzle 48
TEETH	HONEY	SILLY

Puzzle 50	Puzzle 52	Puzzle 54
CHAIR	FERRY	KNEEL

Puzzle 56
WAIST

Puzzle 58
CELLO

Puzzle 60
SCARF

Puzzle 62
MELON

Puzzle 64
RELAX

Puzzle 66
CLOCK

Puzzle 68
LORRY

Puzzle 70
WHALE

Puzzle 72
SHIRT
Hint: an item
of clothing

Puzzle 74
QUIET
Hint: a describing
word (adjective)

Puzzle 76
HEDGE
Hint: found in
the countryside

Puzzle 78
PAINT
Hint: to do with
hobbies or sports

Puzzle 80
SHARK
Hint: a type
of animal

Puzzle 82
TRUCK
Hint: a type
of transport

Puzzle 84
WINDY
Hint: a describing
word (adjective)

Puzzle 86
SPEAK
Hint: a doing or
action word (verb)

Puzzle 88
PHONE
Hint: found in
your house

Puzzle 90
NOISY
Hint: a describing
word (adjective)

Puzzle 92
CANOE
Hint: to do with
hobbies or sports

Puzzle 94
SUGAR
Hint: a type of
food or drink

Puzzle 96
SHELF
Hint: found in
your house

Puzzle 98
CLIMB
Hint: a doing or
action word (verb)

Puzzle 100
RUGBY
Hint: to do with
hobbies or sports

Puzzle 102
KOALA
Hint: a type
of animal

Puzzle 104
ACORN
Hint: found in the
countryside

Puzzle 106
KEBAB
Hint: a type of
food or drink

Puzzle 108
BANJO
Hint: to do
with music

Puzzle 110
WRIST
Hint: a part
of the body

Puzzle 112
CHORD
Hint: to do
with music

Puzzle 114
TOUGH
Hint: a describing
word (adjective)

Puzzle 116
CHOIR
Hint: to do
with music

Puzzle 118
SWAMP
Hint: found in
the countryside

Puzzle 120
VIPER
Hint: a type
of animal

Puzzle 122
FLAME

Puzzle 124
PARTY

Puzzle 126
SMILE

Puzzle 128
WATER

Puzzle 130
THICK

Puzzle 132
GIANT

Puzzle 134
QUEEN

Puzzle 136
MATHS

Puzzle 138
DRONE

Puzzle 140
FRESH

SCORE SHEET

PLAYER 1

PLAYER 2